WINTERTIME
WARM AND COZY TREATS AN

table of contents

© Disney Enterprises, Inc. *Disney FamilyFun* is a trademark of Disney Enterprises, Inc.
For more great ideas, subscribe to *FamilyFun* **magazine at www.familyfun.com/magazine.**
Published by Dalmatian Press, LLC, in conjunction with Disney FamilyFun Group. **Printed in China.**
The Dalmatian Press name is a trademark of Dalmatian Press, Franklin, Tennessee 37067. 1-866-418-2572.
No part of this book may be reproduced or copied in any form without the written permission from the copyright
owner. All rights reserved.   CE14248 Disney FamilyFun Wintertime Fun Warm and Cozy Treats and Crafts

defrosty the snowman

MAKES: 16 SNOWMEN | **PREP TIME:** 30 MINUTES

This wistful snowman appears to be going the way of winter, and we have a feeling he'll soon disappear altogether. He's made from a puddle of white candy melts (one 14-ounce package makes 16 snowmen). For each one, you'll also need 6 mini chocolate chips, a light cocoa candy melt, and a Hershey's Rolo. To make the nose, cut the orange section from a candy corn, then slice it in half lengthwise. Roll the piece between your fingers to form a carrot shape. To assemble your snowman, melt the white candy in a bowl according to the package instructions, then scoop a rounded tablespoon onto a sheet of wax paper. With the back of a spoon, smear the candy into a puddle. Working quickly, press on the light cocoa candy melt, dab a dot of white melted candy, then place the Rolo on top. Finally, add the candy corn nose and mini chocolate chip eyes and mouth.

doughnut snowmen

PREP TIME: 10 MINUTES EACH

No snow? No problem. Whether you live in a Sun Belt state or a wintry clime, your kids can easily build their own mini versions of Frosty. First, set a powdered doughnut hole atop a mini powdered doughnut. (For a taller version, use a pretzel stick or a potato stick to secure a second doughnut hole atop the first.) Use decorators' gel to add a face, buttons, and a carrot nose. (If the gel does not stick, try smoothing the powder with a dab of water first.) To add a top hat to a shorter snowman, stick a small piece of a pretzel or potato stick through a Haviland Thin Mint and into a Reese's Peanut Butter Cup miniature, then secure the hat in place on the snowman. Place on a bed of powered sugar snow!

snowman on a stick

PREP TIME: 5 MINUTES EACH

These banana-based snowmen are decidedly more tropical than the frosty variety. Kids can assemble their own if you prepare the fruit for them. For each snowman, you will need three thick slices of banana, a grape, a sliver of carrot, and a triangular piece of apple. (Tip: Poke a hole in the apple piece with a bamboo skewer first to make assembly easier.) Have your kids slide the fruit onto the skewer, then use the carrot slivers for noses, mini chocolate chips for eyes and buttons, and pretzel sticks for arms.

groundhog day cupcake

On February 2, a certain groundhog in Pennsylvania will emerge from his winter burrow. Legend says an early spring is on its way if he doesn't see his shadow, but it's six more weeks of winter if he does. Whatever Punxsutawney Phil predicts, your kids will surely dig this adorable Groundhog Cupcake.

INGREDIENTS

- ❑ Baked cupcake
- ❑ Almond Joy candy bar
- ❑ White frosting
- ❑ White jelly beans
- ❑ Black decorators' gel
- ❑ Watermelon or peach slice candy
- ❑ Brown M&M's Minis
- ❑ Chocolate cookie

1. Cut out and remove a piece of cake the width of an Almond Joy candy bar from the center of a baked cupcake. Spread a layer of white frosting on the cupcake, then set the candy upright in the hole.

2. For the groundhog's eyes, trim the ends from a white jelly bean, adhere them in place with frosting, then dot them with black decorators' gel. Add a tiny triangle cut from a watermelon or peach slice candy for a nose, brown M&M's Minis for ears and cheeks, and a tiny rectangular piece of white jelly bean for teeth. Sprinkle chocolate cookie crumbs around the partially emerged groundhog, and he's ready to greet his fans.

frosty the cupcake

Snow or no snow, your family can bring winter fun indoors with a band of these merry marshmallow snowmen. For each one, first frost a cooled cupcake (baked from your favorite recipe) with white icing. Next, flatten a large marshmallow on waxed paper with the palm of your hand. Cut a second marshmallow in half horizontally, then stack the halves on the first marshmallow to form a torso and head. Push a thin pretzel stick down through the snowman (this will help him stand up), then set him on the cupcake. Use decorators' gel to create a mouth, eyes, and buttons, then add pretzel stick arms and a wedge cut from an orange slice candy for a nose. Finally, accessorize with a candy hat (a Junior Mint secured to a Thin Mint with icing) and a fruit leather scarf.

jolly snowman bread

MAKES: 4 SNOWMEN | PREP TIME: 45 MINUTES | RISE TIME: 90 MINUTES/30–45 MINUTES | BAKE TIME: 30 MINUTES

Invite your kids to shape this classic white bread dough into snowmen. When the snowmen are baked, the kids can tie on ribbon scarves and present their edible sculptures to teachers and friends.

INGREDIENTS

- ❑ 5½ cups all-purpose flour
- ❑ 2 tablespoons brown sugar
- ❑ 2 teaspoons salt
- ❑ ½ cup warm water
- ❑ 1 (¼-ounce) package active dry yeast
- ❑ Pinch of sugar
- ❑ 1½ cups warm milk
- ❑ 4 tablespoons softened butter
- ❑ Raisins, dried apricots, gumdrops

1. In a large mixing bowl, combine the flour, brown sugar, and salt. Set aside. Pour the warm water (around 100°) into a large bowl and sprinkle in the yeast and a pinch of sugar. Stir and let the mix sit for 5 minutes, until bubbles begin to appear. Stir in the warm milk, butter, and 2 cups of the dry ingredients. Stir in the remaining dry ingredients 1 cup at a time, mixing until the dough is stiff.

2. Turn the dough out onto a lightly floured countertop and knead for 5 to 10 minutes or until the dough becomes smooth and springs when touched. Grease a large mixing bowl, place the dough in the bowl, and cover it with a dish towel. Let the dough rise for about 1½ hours or until doubled in bulk.

3. Punch down the risen dough and turn it out onto a lightly floured countertop. Divide it into 4 pieces (1 for each snowman). Cut off the top third of each piece and shape it into the snowman's head; shape the larger piece into a ball for the body. Place the 2 balls on a baking sheet and pinch them together. Repeat with the remaining 3 pieces of dough until you have 4 snowmen. Cover and let them rise for 30 to 45 minutes.

4. Heat the oven to 350°. Brush the snowmen with milk and adorn with raisin eyes, a dried apricot nose, and gumdrop buttons. Cover the fruit and gumdrops with small pieces of aluminum foil so they won't burn, then bake for 30 minutes or until golden brown. Cool on racks. Tie a ribbon around each snowman's neck for a scarf. To present, wrap in plastic before adding the scarf.

polar bear family

MAKES: 3 TREATS | PREP TIME: 20 MINUTES

We just couldn't bear to keep this cool polar family a secret any longer. Here's how to make your own irresistible trio, starting with Mama Bear.

INGREDIENTS

- Light-colored cupcakes, 1 regular and 3 mini
- White frosting
- Shredded coconut
- 3 large and 2 small white gumdrops
- 1 Junior Mint candy
- Chocolate chips, 4 regular and 4 mini

1. First, frost the top, sides, and bottoms of both a regular-size cupcake and a mini cupcake with white frosting. For each cupcake, frost the bottom first; then use a fork stuck into the bottom to hold the cupcake while you frost the rest of it. Roll the cupcakes in shredded coconut, then, working on waxed paper, set the cupcakes on their sides with the top of the smaller cupcake stuck to the bottom of the larger one to form the bear's head.

2. Add 2 horizontal slices from a large white gumdrop for ears, a Junior Mint candy for a nose, and 2 chocolate chips for eyes. For each cub, frost a mini cupcake and a large gumdrop, then roll them in coconut and arrange them on their sides. Add 2 horizontal slices from a small white gumdrop for ears, a chocolate chip nose, and 2 mini chocolate chip eyes.

merry marshmallows

MAKES: 24 | **PREP TIME:** 40 MINUTES | **COOL TIME:** 12 HOURS

Top your cocoa with these festive homemade treats. Your kids may be amazed to learn that a few simple ingredients and a cookie cutter are all it takes to create their own marshmallows in fun shapes. Paired with hot cocoa, they'll make a perfect treat on any cold winter's night.

INGREDIENTS

- ❏ ⅓ cup cold water
- ❏ 2 envelopes unflavored gelatin
- ❏ 1½ cups sugar
- ❏ ¼ cup water
- ❏ ¼ cup corn syrup
- ❏ Pinch of salt
- ❏ ½ teaspoon vanilla extract
- ❏ Confectioners' sugar
- ❏ Colored sugar

1. First, pour the ⅓ cup of cold water into a large mixing bowl, sprinkle the gelatin over it, and set it aside.

2. Combine the sugar, ¼ cup of water, corn syrup, and salt in a medium saucepan over medium heat, stirring until dissolved. Stop stirring and heat the mixture (adults only) until it boils and reaches 240° on a candy thermometer.

3. Carefully pour the hot syrup (again, a parent's job) over the gelatin and beat with an electric mixer on high speed for 12 minutes. Blend in the vanilla extract, then scrape the batter into a 9x13-inch pan lightly coated with cooking spray.

4. Let the marshmallows sit until they're dry to the touch (this may take up to 12 hours depending on the humidity in your area). Invert the pan onto a cutting board dusted with confectioners' sugar. Pour the colored sugar onto a plate or shallow dish, then use 2-inch cookie cutters to cut the marshmallow into shapes. Press the top of each marshmallow into the colored sugar. Store in an airtight container. Makes twenty-four 2-inch marshmallows.

cub cakes

PREP TIME: 20

Your cubs will make tracks for the kitchen when they spy these paw-print cupcakes. Beware—cub cakes walk away from kitchens fast.

INGREDIENTS

- ❏ Cupcakes
- ❏ White or light chocolate frosting
- ❏ Mint patties
- ❏ Junior Mints or chocolate chips

1. To make these treats, frost your favorite cupcakes with white or light chocolate icing (for a furry paw, mix the frosting with grated coconut first).

2. Top each cupcake with a small mint patty. Then place three Junior Mints or chocolate chips, points up, around the larger patty for claw marks.

caramel apple cider

MAKES: 4 | **PREP TIME:** 20 MINUTES

Warm up a cold day with a mug of hot cider topped with a hint of caramel.

INGREDIENTS

Cider
- ☐ ¼ cup heavy cream
- ☐ ¼ cup brown sugar
- ☐ 3 cups apple cider
- ☐ ½ cup water

Caramel Whipped Cream
- ☐ ½ cup heavy cream
- ☐ 1 tablespoon brown sugar

1. Bring the cream and brown sugar to a boil in a medium saucepan over medium heat. Stir in the cider and the water and raise the heat to medium high, heating just until the cider begins to steam, about 4 minutes. Set aside.

2. Caramel Whipped Cream: In a small chilled bowl, whip the heavy cream with the brown sugar until soft peaks form.

3. Divide the cider among 4 mugs, top each one with 2 tablespoons of caramel whipped cream and serve immediately.

penguin cupcakes

MAKES: 24 CUPCAKES | **PREP TIME:** 40 MINUTES | **BAKE TIME:** PER MIX

Waddle you want for a snow day snack? How about one of these friendly fellows?

INGREDIENTS

- ☐ Vanilla cupcakes
- ☐ Vanilla frosting
- ☐ Chocolate cookies (we used Keebler Fudge Shoppe Grasshopper Fudge Mint Cookies— 3 halves per penguin for body and head)
- ☐ Dried apricots (cut into triangles for the beak and feet)
- ☐ Brown M&M's Minis (eyes)

1. Have your child help make a batch of vanilla cupcakes with vanilla frosting. Use your favorite recipe or 1 box of cake mix, which will make 24 cupcakes. Buy or make 2 to 3 cups of frosting (save some for decorating glue).

2. Decorate as shown, cutting the cookies in half with a knife (a parent's job) and using extra frosting to attach the apricot beak and the M&M's eyes.

hot chocolate mug cakes

MAKES: ABOUT 12 MUGS | **PREP TIME:** 30 MINUTES | **BAKE TIME:** PER MIX

Bake your favorite chocolate cake batter in clear individual mugs for a warming winter dessert. Simply coat the insides of oven-safe mugs with cooking spray, then fill the mugs halfway with chocolate cake batter. We used a mix for German chocolate cake, which is a lighter color than regular chocolate cake and looks more like hot cocoa. Follow the cupcake baking instructions on the cake mix package. The cakes are done when a toothpick inserted into the center of one comes out clean or with just a few crumbs. Allow the cakes to cool for about 15 minutes. Top each mug with a generous dollop of marshmallow creme and serve with a spoon. One cake mix makes enough batter for 12 of our mugs; if you want fewer than a dozen, bake the remaining batter in a small pan.

meringue snowflakes

MAKES: 20 | **PREP TIME:** 40 MINUTES | **BAKE TIME:** 1 HOUR

Presented in decorative tins, these sparkly meringues are satisfying both to make and to give. And you don't have to stick to the snowflake design; the meringue can be piped into snowmen, letters, hearts or just about any shape you like. Tip: For the best results, avoid making them on a humid day.

INGREDIENTS

- ❑ 2 large egg whites,
  at room temperature
- ❑ ½ teaspoon cream of tartar
- ❑ 1 cup confectioners' sugar
- ❑ ¼ teaspoon flavored extract, such as
  lemon, peppermint, orange, or almond
- ❑ 2 tablespoons colored sugar or
  edible glitter

1. Heat the oven to 200°. In a large bowl, using an electric mixer on medium speed, beat the egg whites and cream of tartar until frothy, about 3 minutes. Set the mixer speed to high and beat another 3 minutes or so until the egg whites are fluffy.

2. Add the confectioners' sugar, 1 table-spoon at a time, and continue beating until the egg whites are stiff and glossy, about 5 minutes. Then beat in the extract.

3. Line 2 large baking sheets with parchment paper. Use a pencil to draw 4-inch snowflake patterns on the paper. The meringues will not spread, so they can be drawn fairly close together. Turn the papers printed-side down and stick them to the baking sheets by dabbing a little meringue in each corner.

4. Spoon the meringue into a large pastry bag fitted with a ¼-inch round tip and pipe it, erring on the thick side so the snowflakes will be less fragile, onto the paper-lined sheets following the patterns. Sprinkle the meringues with colored sugar or edible glitter. Bake the snowflakes until dry but not browned, about 1 hour. Carefully slide the parchment paper from the baking sheets to wire racks and let the meringues cool completely.

5. Using clean scissors, cut the paper between the meringues to separate them. Then gently peel away the paper from each one, keeping one hand under the snowflake to support the edges. The meringues will stay crisp for up to 2 weeks if stored in an airtight container at room temperature (do not refrigerate them).

chocolate-drizzled trail mix

MAKES: 12 SERVINGS | **PREP TIME:** 12 MINUTES

When kids snack on trail mix from the store, many go right for the chocolate pieces and ignore the rest. But in this ingenious recipe, melted chocolate is poured over the nuts, seeds, and fruit, so the kids eat all the goodness instead of just picking out the goodies. (Keep hand wipes handy to help tidy chocolaty fingers.) To make a batch, mix together 3 cups nuts (we used peanuts, almonds, and pecans), ½ cup sunflower seeds, ½ cup coconut flakes, 1 cup raisins, and ½ cup dried cranberries or cherries. Spread the mixture on a baking sheet lined with waxed paper. Melt 1 cup chocolate chips in a microwave. Pour the chocolate over the baking sheet in ribbons. Stir to coat everything. Let the chocolate cool, then break the mix into pieces and pack it in individual containers.

snowy trail mix

MAKES: 10 CUPS | **PREP TIME:** 20 MINUTES | **COOL TIME:** 20 MINUTES

With its sweet "snow" coating, this mix is a great snack for a winter outing. In a large bowl, mix together 3 cups pretzel sticks, 1½ cups corn cereal (we used Crispix), ¾ cup pecan halves, ½ cup cashews, and ½ cup dried cranberries. Melt 12 ounces of white chocolate according to the package directions and slowly pour it over the mix, stirring gently. Scoop the mix onto waxed paper to cool, about 20 minutes, then break it into bite-size clumps.

scrumptious pretzels

MAKES: 6 PRETZELS | **PREP TIME:** 30/30 MINUTES | **RISE TIME:** 45 MINUTES | **BAKE TIME:** 12-15 MINUTES PER BATCH

Aspiring young bakers will love our twist on this classic snack. With their fresh-baked aroma, chewy texture, and salted tops, soft pretzels make a satisfying snack for kids and adults alike. For variety, try one of our flavored pretzels—cinnamon sugar or pizza.

INGREDIENTS

- ❏ 1¼ cups lukewarm water
- ❏ 1 (¼-ounce) packet active dry yeast (2¼ teaspoons)
- ❏ 1 tablespoon light brown sugar
- ❏ 1½ teaspoons salt
- ❏ 3¼ cups unbleached bread flour

- ❏ ¼ cup hot water
- ❏ 1 teaspoon sugar
- ❏ 3 tablespoons unsalted butter, melted

Optional
- ❏ Coarse or Kosher salt
- ❏ Cinnamon sugar
- ❏ Sun-dried-tomato pesto
- ❏ Parmesan cheese

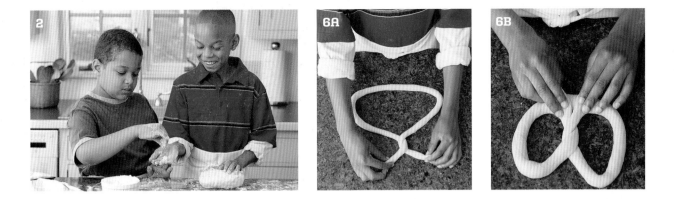

1. Pour the lukewarm water into a large mixing bowl and sprinkle on the yeast. Wait 5 minutes, then stir in the brown sugar, salt, and 2 cups of the flour. Stir the mixture vigorously with a wooden spoon for about 100 strokes.

2. Gradually stir in enough of the remaining flour, ¼ cup at a time, to make a semifirm dough. Turn the dough out onto a floured surface and knead it for 7 to 8 minutes, dusting the surface with flour to keep the dough from sticking.

3. Place the dough in a lightly oiled bowl and roll it around to coat its entire surface. Cover the bowl with plastic wrap and set it in a warm place until the dough is nearly doubled in volume, about 45 minutes. Meanwhile, lightly grease a large, heavy, shiny (not dark) baking sheet with vegetable shortening.

4. Turn the dough out onto a flour-dusted surface and knead for 1 minute. Divide the dough in half, placing half back in the bowl and re-covering it with plastic wrap.

5. Divide the other half of the dough into 3 equal pieces. Shape each into a ball and let them rest for 5 minutes on a flour-dusted surface. Then roll each ball under your palms and outstretched fingers until it's about 3 feet long and ½ inch thick.

6. Heat the oven to 450°. Shape the ropes of dough by making a circle and twisting the ends (as shown above in step 6A). Fold the ends back over the circle and pinch the dough (step 6B). After shaping the pretzels, place them on the baking sheet, leaving plenty of space between them.

7. Stir the hot water and sugar together in a small bowl. Using a pastry brush, lightly brush the water mixture over the pretzels. Top them with a bit of coarse salt, if desired. (Options: Sprinkle with cinnamon sugar; or, brush on a tablespoon of sun-dried-tomato pesto.) Set the pretzels aside for 10 minutes.

8. Bake the pretzels on the center oven rack until golden brown, about 12 to 15 minutes, rotating the sheet 180 degrees halfway through the baking. Start shaping the other half of the dough into 3 more pretzels.

9. Place a sheet of plastic wrap or aluminum foil under a wire rack and transfer the baked pretzels to the rack. Using a pastry brush, apply melted butter liberally over the pretzels; this makes them soft and flavorful. (Options: Sprinkle on more cinnamon sugar; or, shake on Parmesan cheese.) Let the pretzels cool briefly, but enjoy them while they're warm.

glittery window clings

Let the sun shine in through a few of these glittery window clings. They stick to glass and plastic but, unlike real snow, they are easy to remove!

YOU WILL NEED

- Paper and pencil
- Cookie sheet
- Waxed paper
- Dimensional fabric paint (we used Scribbles brand in Glittering Crystal)

1. Draw a snowflake template (small, compact designs work best), or download ours at **FamilyFun.com/magazine.** Lay the template faceup on the cookie sheet and cover it with the waxed paper.

2. Using a thin line of the fabric paint (approximately ⅛-inch wide), trace the snowflake design on the waxed paper as shown, making sure all of the paint lines connect. Let the window cling dry overnight, then carefully peel it from the waxed paper.

let-it-snow t-shirt

Making this one-of-a-kind tee involves some waiting time, so it's a perfect craft for sleepovers or winter break.

YOU WILL NEED

❑ Black marker
❑ Paper
❑ Cardboard
❑ White cotton shirt
❑ Tacky glue
❑ Sponge brush (or a new kitchen sponge)
❑ Fabric paint

1. Use a black marker to draw a thick-lined snowflake template on the paper, or download ours at **FamilyFun.com/magazine.**

2. Place the template over the cardboard and slip both inside the shirt, centering them behind the upper front of the garment. You should be able to see the template through the shirt.

3. Using a thin line of tacky glue (about ¼-inch wide), trace the snowflake design onto the shirt. Let it dry for 10 minutes, then fill in any gaps with additional glue. Let the glue dry completely, until it is transparent (approximately 3 hours).

4. Dip the sponge brush in the paint and dab around the snowflake, completely covering the surrounding area. Use less paint toward the outer edge of the design. Let the paint dry overnight.

5. Soak the tee in warm water for about 10 minutes or until the glue softens. Peel off the glue and let the shirt dry, then follow the package instructions to set the fabric paint.

penguin parade

Transform used soda or water bottles and your child's lone socks into playful penguins.

YOU WILL NEED

- ❑ Black and white glossy acrylic paint
- ❑ Plastic soda or water bottles (we used 12-ounce, 1-liter, and 2-liter bottles)
- ❑ Styrofoam balls (2- to 3-inch diameter)
- ❑ Black and yellow craft foam sheets
- ❑ Tacky glue
- ❑ Masking tape (optional)
- ❑ Butter knife
- ❑ Googly eyes (we used ¾- to 1-inch diameter)
- ❑ Funnel
- ❑ Sand
- ❑ Small doll accessories
- ❑ Child's socks

1. For each penguin, pour two parts black paint and one part water inside a bottle (we used 1 to 4 tablespoons of paint depending on the size of the bottle). Screw on the cap and shake the bottle to coat the sides. Remove the cap and save it for later.

2. On the outside of the bottle, paint a white oval from the spout to the bottom. Dry overnight (the inside may be slightly wet in the morning).

3. Coat a Styrofoam ball with black paint and let it dry.

4. Cut two wings from the black craft foam and a beak and feet from the yellow craft foam (you can download our templates from **FamilyFun. com/magazine**). Glue the wings and feet to the bottle as shown and let them dry. If needed, use masking tape to hold the wings in place as they dry.

5. With the knife, bore a hole in the Styrofoam ball big enough to fit the neck of the bottle. Glue on googly eyes. Make a small slit below the eyes, insert a few dabs of glue, then slide the beak into the opening.

6. Funnel sand into the bottle to weigh it down (we used 1 to 2 cups depending on the bottle's size). Replace the cap and press the Styrofoam head on top.

7. Dress the penguin in doll accessories or use kids' socks to make your own. For a hat, snip a 6- to 8-inch length from a sock and knot one end. For a scarf, cut a 1½-inch-wide loop from a sock, snip it open, and fringe the ends.

sparkling ice crystals

String up a few of these crystals, made of pipe cleaners and beads, and get ready for a flurry of compliments. For a cool twist, use silver pipe cleaners and pom-poms.

YOU WILL NEED

❏ 12-inch white iridescent pipe cleaners
❏ Clear tri or sunburst beads
❏ Needle and fishing line
❏ White iridescent pom-poms

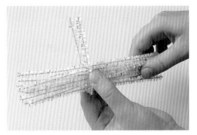

1. Cut 6 pipe cleaners in half to create 12 pieces. Hold 11 pieces together and tightly wrap the last piece around the middle of the bundle, as shown, twisting its ends to secure it.

2. Spread the pipe cleaner pieces into a starburst shape and thread about 5 beads onto each pipe cleaner half as shown.

3. Using the needle, thread the pom-poms on the fishing line, then tie the snowflake to one end of the line.

frosty the doorstop

While most snowmen are made up of flakes, ours is made from a single paving stone. Want your Frosty to greet folks from the porch? Use all-weather paint instead of acrylic.

YOU WILL NEED

- ❏ Keyhole-shaped paver (available at many home improvement stores)
- ❏ Paintbrush
- ❏ White and black acrylic paint
- ❏ Orange modeling clay
- ❏ Super glue
- ❏ Fleece
- ❏ Pipe cleaner
- ❏ Two 1½-inch pom-poms
- ❏ Rubber band
- ❏ Felt

1. Rinse off the paver to remove any loose bits of dirt or cement. Paint it white and let it dry. If needed, apply a second coat and let it dry completely.

2. Lay the paver flat and paint on the eyes, mouth, and buttons. Let the face dry, then mold a clay nose and affix it with super glue (a parent's job).

3. Cut a fleece scarf (ours measures 1 by 22 inches) and tie it in place. For the earmuffs, bend a 5-inch piece of pipe cleaner into an arc. Super glue the ends to either side of the head and the pom-poms over the ends (a parent's job), then wrap the rubber band around the snowman's head to hold the earmuffs in place until the glue dries.

4. To protect indoor floors, super-glue a small piece of felt to the base of the snowman.

melty the snowman

This whimsical windowsill decoration serves as a sign of spring no matter what climate you live in. To make one, cut a puddle shape from white felt and use tacky glue to attach a white pom-pom to the top. With black puffy paint, add eyes, a mouth, and buttons. Glue on a craft foam nose and twig arms. As an added feature, wrap a felt scarf around Melty's neck and glue it in place.

sock snowfolk

These snuggly snowfolk make a great craft for a chilly day. For each one, first pour ½ cup of dried beans or rice into a clean, empty plastic container, such as a single-serving milk bottle, a water bottle, or a plastic peanut jar (ours were about 7 to 10 inches tall). Turn a white tube sock inside out and slide it over the bottle, starting at the bottom. Tuck the top of the sock inside the bottle, trimming it a bit first if necessary.

For a hat, cut a piece of colored fleece that's at least half as tall as the bottle and wide enough to wrap around it with at least 1 inch of overlap. Wrap the fleece around the top half of the bottle and secure it with a rubber band or elastic hair tie near the bottom of the fleece. Gather the material at the top of the hat and secure it with another rubber band or hair tie, as shown at right. To add a pom-pom to the hat, remove the fleece from the bottle, turn it inside out, then rubber-band it back in place and hot-glue a pom-pom to the top. Roll up the bottom edge of the hat or tuck it under for a brim.

Next, hot-glue on the snowman's features: a carrot nose (half an orange pipe cleaner coiled around the tip of a sharpened pencil to form a cone), small black button eyes, and colorful buttons down his front. Finally, tie on a strip of fleece for a scarf.

birdseed biscuit

Keep an eye out for feathered friends this winter. The Great Backyard Bird Count is in February, when people across the country spend 15 minutes or more taking stock of the birds in their towns. For tips, tally sheets, and events, go to **birdsource.org/gbbc.**

To encourage birds to visit your yard, try hanging a homemade birdseed biscuit. Our recipe makes two 3-inch biscuits (one is shown here) or a single 4-inch biscuit. Mix together ¾ cup of birdseed, 1 tablespoon of flour, and 2 tablespoons of water. Spray or wipe a cookie cutter with oil and place it on a foil-covered cookie sheet. Pack the mixture into the cutter, inserting half a straw near the top to create a hole for hanging. Bake the biscuit (with the straw) in a 170° oven until the biscuit is hard, about one hour. Let it cool. Remove the straw, thread a ribbon through the hole, and hang it outside in a sheltered spot.

winter sun catcher

This eye-catching ornament strikes a festive note, and it's a great yard decoration too. Make it a day or two ahead so it will have plenty of time to freeze. Feel free to improvise with any colorful natural materials you have on hand.

YOU WILL NEED

❑ Disposable foil pan (we used a rectangular cake pan)

❑ One orange cut into rounds

❑ A few small pine branches

❑ Fresh or frozen cranberries

❑ Sturdy twine, cut into 4 lengths (ours were about 2 feet each)

1. Place the pan on a flat surface. Arrange the orange rounds and pine branches in the pan and add enough water to cover them. Sprinkle on the berries.

2. For the hanging cords, lay one end of each piece of twine in the pan, submerging it at least several inches. Let the pan freeze outside (or place it in the freezer).

3. Remove the ice block from the pan (run warm water over the back if needed) and hang it up outside.

ice candle

In this classic kitchen craft, kids (with a parent's help) can combine ice and hot wax to form a cool, lacy-looking candle. Set it in the center of your table to add a special wintertime glow.

YOU WILL NEED

- ❑ Scissors
- ❑ Cylindrical cardboard container (salt or oatmeal)
- ❑ Paper towel
- ❑ Cooking oil
- ❑ Knife
- ❑ White tapered candle
- ❑ Large tin can
- ❑ 1 pound of paraffin wax
- ❑ Large saucepan
- ❑ Wooden skewer
- ❑ Crayon pieces
- ❑ Large spoon
- ❑ Crushed ice
- ❑ Bowl

1. Have your child prepare a mold by cutting off the top of the cardboard container. Use a paper towel to coat the inside with cooking oil. With a knife, trim the bottom from the taper so the taper is the same height as the mold.

2. Meanwhile, fill the tin can with the wax. Then place it in a saucepan filled with 2 inches of water and set the pan over low heat. Use a wooden skewer to stir the melting wax. Mix in crayon pieces to get your desired candle color.

3. Pour ½ inch of wax into the prepared mold and immediately stick the taper into the center, wick end up. Hold the taper in place for a minute or two while the wax sets.

4. Spoon 2 inches of crushed ice around the taper, then cover the ice almost completely with melted wax. Add more ice, then more wax, alternating until the mold is filled.

5. Set the mold in a bowl for about an hour (it will leak water), letting the wax harden completely, then peel off the cardboard.

cornstarch-clay creations

This recipe yields enough for two kids to each make a sculpture or two, but if friends are over (as they often are on winter weekends), definitely double the ingredient amounts.

YOU WILL NEED

❏ ⅔ cup salt
❏ ⅓ cup baking soda
❏ ½ cup cornstarch
❏ decorative hardware

1. In a small saucepan, mix the salt and baking soda with ⅓ cup of water and bring to a boil.

2. In a small bowl, combine the cornstarch and ¼ cup of water and stir well.

3. When the salt mixture boils, remove it from the heat and add the cornstarch mixture. Stir vigorously for a minute or two to thicken the clay. Spoon it onto a sheet of waxed paper and allow it to cool before working with it.

4. Shape into little snowmen, angels, and animals.

5. Put out decorative "stick-ons" in little bowls or paper cups to add fun embellishments, such as sequins, googly eyes, tacks, keys, cup hooks, soda-can tabs, nuts, bolts, washers, and screws. The end piece from a lamp pull-chain makes a nice bell to hang on a deer's neck.

6. Place the creations on a cookie sheet covered with waxed paper to dry overnight.

tabletop ice hockey

Your kids can get plenty of ice time (no pads or helmets required) when they face-off on this miniature rink, complete with goals, tiny hockey sticks, and real ice.

To start, make the goals by cutting a plastic berry basket in quarters. Slide one piece inside another and secure it in place with craft glue.

For the rink, cut a piece of white low- or medium-tack Con-Tact paper to fit the bottom of a shallow, freezer-safe baking pan. With a ruler and red and blue permanent markers, draw lines across the paper as shown. Trace around the rim of a disposable cup for the circles. Add a dot to the center of each circle. Now remove the backing from the paper and stick it to the pan. Fill the pan partway with water. Set the goals in place and put it in the freezer. Allow the ice to freeze overnight or until solid.

For 2 hockey sticks, use a craft knife (parents only) to make an angled cut 1 inch from each end of a craft stick. Glue each of the short pieces to a full craft stick as shown, then wrap them with narrow strips of colored tape.

When the ice has set, remove the pan from the freezer, grab a button for a puck, and have 2 players face-off at center ice!

red goal line
blue line at one third of sheet
red dashed center line
blue line at two thirds of sheet
red goal line
red referee crease
blue center ice spot and circle
4 red faceoff spots and circles

pipe cleaner penguins

Create your own march of the penguins by crafting a group of these adorable cold-climate creatures. You can make adults with the directions below or cut the pipe cleaners in half to make baby birds.

1. Make a body by coiling a 12-inch black pipe cleaner around a pencil. Hook a 2½-inch piece of white pipe cleaner between the top third and fourth coils and around the bottom coil.

2. For each wing, fold a 4-inch piece of black pipe cleaner in half and bend the ends. Attach it by tucking the bent ends between the top third and fourth coils.

3. Cut a beak and feet from orange craft foam. Stick the beak between the coils and secure it with a dot of craft glue. Then glue on the feet and a pair of googly eyes.

When winter's cold settles over the land, mama and papa creatures know what they must do to survive with their young: they gather pipe cleaners, foam balls, and colorful pins and get to work crafting. In just minutes, a cooped-up family can assemble all manner of animal friends and magical snowmen, and bring some light to the season's darkness.

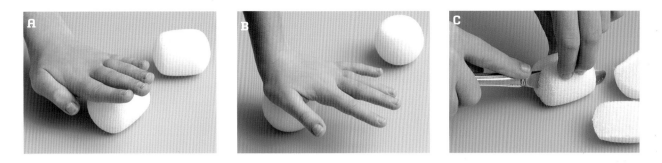

HOW TO MAKE A WOODLAND SNOW SCENE

1. For each creature, cut the white pipe cleaners to the lengths indicated. Group them by length.

2. Fold or shape the pipe cleaner parts. Using the photos as a guide, bend the ears, feet, and tail and, if needed, twist together the neck, legs, wings, and antlers.

3. Shape and cut the Styrofoam balls. Depending on the project, you may need to roll the balls with your palm (A), flatten them (B), or slice them with a butter knife (C) for arms or legs.

4. Assemble the creature as shown in the diagram. Simply insert the shaped pipe cleaner parts or connectors into the foam.

5. Insert colored-ball-head straight pins to create eyes, a nose, and other features. If the pins are longer than the diameter of the animal's head, insert them so their points extend into the neck.

6. Drape white felt over stacked, flat objects (such as books) to create a snowy base. Arrange your woodland scene.

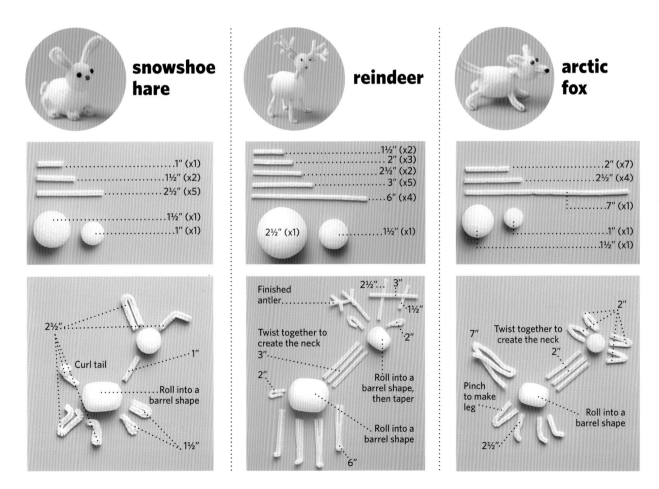

snowshoe hare

.....1" (x1)
.....1½" (x2)
.....2½" (x5)

.....1½" (x1)
.....1" (x1)

2½"
Curl tail
1"
Roll into a barrel shape
1½"

reindeer

1½" (x2)
2" (x3)
2½" (x2)
3" (x5)
6" (x4)

2½" (x1)
1½" (x1)

Finished antler
2½"..... 3"
1½"
Twist together to create the neck
3"
2"
2"
Roll into a barrel shape, then taper
Roll into a barrel shape
6"

arctic fox

2" (x7)
2½" (x4)
7" (x1)

1" (x1)
1½" (x1)

7"
Twist together to create the neck
2"
2"
Pinch to make leg
Roll into a barrel shape
2½"

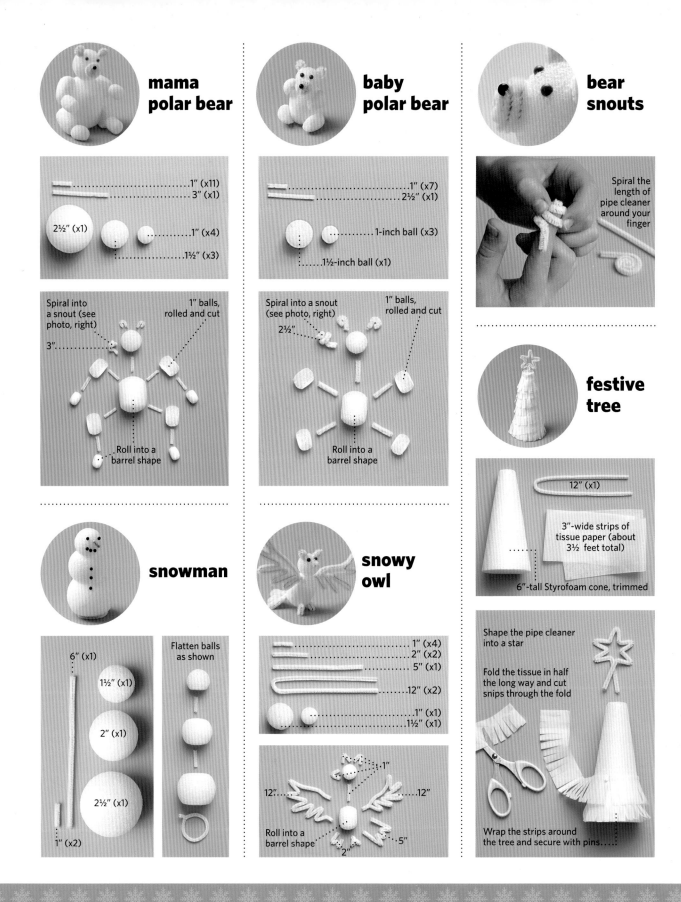

mama polar bear

1" (x11)
3" (x1)
2½" (x1)
1" (x4)
1½" (x3)

Spiral into a snout (see photo, right)

3"

1" balls, rolled and cut

Roll into a barrel shape

baby polar bear

1" (x7)
2½" (x1)
1-inch ball (x3)
1½-inch ball (x1)

Spiral into a snout (see photo, right)

2½"

1" balls, rolled and cut

Roll into a barrel shape

bear snouts

Spiral the length of pipe cleaner around your finger

festive tree

12" (x1)

3"-wide strips of tissue paper (about 3½ feet total)

6"-tall Styrofoam cone, trimmed

Shape the pipe cleaner into a star

Fold the tissue in half the long way and cut snips through the fold

Wrap the strips around the tree and secure with pins

snowman

6" (x1)
1½" (x1)
2" (x1)
2½" (x1)
1" (x2)

Flatten balls as shown

snowy owl

1" (x4)
2" (x2)
5" (x1)
12" (x2)
1" (x1)
1½" (x1)

Roll into a barrel shape

1"
12"
12"
5"
2"